REPORT

ON THE

RULES AND STATUTES

OF THE OFFICE OF

"PREACHER TO THE UNIVERSITY AND PLUMMER PROFESSOR OF CHRISTIAN MORALS,"

AT

HARVARD COLLEGE,

WITH THE

PROCEEDINGS OF THE OVERSEERS THEREON,

APRIL 12, 1855.

BOSTON:
PRESS OF T. R. MARVIN, 42 CONGRESS STREET.
1855.

REPORT

ON THE

RULES AND STATUTES

OF THE OFFICE OF

"PREACHER TO THE UNIVERSITY AND PLUMMER PROFESSOR OF CHRISTIAN MORALS,"

AT

HARVARD COLLEGE,

WITH THE

PROCEEDINGS OF THE OVERSEERS THEREON,

APRIL 12, 1855.

BOSTON:
PRESS OF T. R. MARVIN, 42 CONGRESS STREET.
1855.

PLUMMER PROFESSORSHIP.

At a Meeting of the BOARD OF OVERSEERS OF HARVARD COLLEGE, held in the Senate Chamber in Boston, on the 12th day of April, 1855, His Excellency the Governor in the chair, the Hon. ROBERT C. WINTHROP presented the following

REPORT.

TO THE HONORABLE AND REVEREND THE BOARD OF OVERSEERS OF HARVARD COLLEGE, THE COMMITTEE TO WHOM WERE REFERRED THE "RULES AND STATUTES OF THE OFFICE OF PREACHER TO THE UNIVERSITY AND PLUMMER PROFESSOR OF CHRISTIAN MORALS," RESPECTFULLY SUBMIT THE FOLLOWING REPORT:

It appears that Miss Caroline Plummer, of Salem, by a codicil to her last Will and Testament, dated 9 March, 1845, made provision for establishing a new Professorship at Harvard College as follows:

"The estate of my late (entirely beloved) brother Ernestus Augustus Plummer, having fallen into my hands for disposal thereof, and I wishing to bequeath it as I think would be most agreeable to his wishes, do now, in fulfillment of what I verily believe would have been his wish, give and bequeath the sum of Twenty-five Thousand Dollars to the President and

Fellows of Harvard College, which I direct to be safely invested and put at interest, and the income thereof to be forever appropriated for the support of a Professor of the Philosophy of the Heart and of the Moral, Physical and Christian Life in Harvard University, whose province it shall be, according to rules and exercises established from time to time by the said President and Fellows, and on the basis of Christian faith and love, to enlighten all who are or may be engaged in the education pursued there, whether governors, instructors or students, in the manner of discharging their respective duties, so as best to promote generous affections, manly virtues and Christian conduct, and more especially, to aid and instruct the students in what most nearly concerns their moral and physical welfare, their health, their good habits, and their Christian character, acting towards them, by personal intercourse and persuasion, the part of a parent, as well as that of a teacher and friend."

It was furthermore provided in the same instrument as follows:

"The Professor shall be of the Christian religion, and a Master of Arts, and bearing the character of a learned, pious, and honest man. He shall be elected by the President and Fellows, and approved by the Overseers of Harvard College for such a term of years as may by them be ordered."

The Testatrix adds: "As a tribute to the memory of my late dear brother, my wish is, that this contemplated Professorship should forever bear his name."

It further appears that, by a subsequent instrument, the amount devoted by Miss Plummer to the purpose thus set forth, was reduced to Fifteen Thousand Dollars.

It appears also, that the Corporation of the College, on the 5th of July last,—the death of Miss Plummer having previously occurred, and the contents of her Will having been communicated to them,—passed the following vote:

"Voted, That the President and Fellows of Harvard College accept the liberal donation of Miss Plummer, upon the terms and conditions, and to the trusts and purposes and intent therein expressed, and that notice thereof be given by the President in suitable terms to the Executor."

It appears, finally, that with a view to carry out and fulfill the provisions and conditions of the foundation thus established on their part, the President and Fellows have adopted, and have now submitted to the Overseers for their approbation, the following Rules and Statutes:

I. The Professor shall be styled "Preacher to the University and Plummer Professor of Christian Morals."

II. To be eligible to this Professorship, the Candidate must be a Master of Arts, and an ordained Minister of the Gospel, bearing the character of a learned, pious and honest man.

III. His duties shall be:

1. To conduct the daily devotions in the College Chapel.

2. To be the preacher and pastor of those who worship in the College Chapel on the Lord's Day.

3. To give such moral and religious instruction to

the undergraduates, whether by lectures or recitations, as shall be agreed upon in the assignment of studies by the College Faculty.

4. By counsel and sympathy, by personal intercourse, occasional voluntary meetings, and other suitable means, to warn and guard the students against the dangers to which they are exposed; to supply, as far as may be, their need of home influences, and to promote among them an earnest Christian faith and life.

IV. It shall be at the option of the Professor, whether to belong to the College Faculty or not.

V. The Professor shall hold his office by the same tenure generally, as the other Professors on foundations, and shall be subject to removal by the President and Fellows for any cause by them deemed just and sufficient, the Overseers consenting thereto.

VI. The President and Fellows, with the concurrence of the Overseers, shall have authority to revise and amend these Rules and Statutes from time to time, as they see fit; provided only, that no changes are introduced inconsistent with the conditions and the general purpose of the foundation.

In the judgment of your Committee, two distinct questions are thus presented for the consideration of the Overseers:

1. Will they concur with the Corporation in establishing a new Professorship, in conformity with the Will of the late Miss Caroline Plummer? and

2. Will they assent to the Rules and Statutes which have been submitted to them by the Corpora-

tion for defining the qualifications and duties, the title and the tenure, of the new Professor?

In the course of their deliberations, the undersigned have found frequent occasion to regret, that any nomination of a candidate for the contemplated Professorship had not been withheld until these questions, or at least the first of them, had been considered and decided by the Overseers. And they trust they shall not be thought wanting in proper respect for the Corporation, if they put upon record, at the outset of their report, a distinct expression of opinion, that the practice which has now been twice repeated within a brief period,—and which may perhaps rest upon a longer usage and upon better reasons than they are aware of,—by which the nomination of a candidate is presented simultaneously with the original proposition for the establishment of a new office, is calculated to create misunderstanding between the two Boards, to embarrass and prejudice the action of the Overseers, and particularly to do injustice to the candidate, who is thus exposed to be held in suspense, and even to be practically rejected, upon grounds entirely independent of his own merits.

Your Committee hope that it may be expressly understood, in the present instance, that the delay of this Board has thus far resulted solely from the desire to discharge their duties deliberately and independently, upon questions of the highest interest and importance, and which are entirely disconnected from any personal considerations whatever.

It would be idle to attempt to disguise the fact, that the proposal to establish a new Religious Professorship at Harvard College, from whatever quarter and under whatever circumstances it may come, is regarded with extreme sensitiveness and jealousy in many parts of the State. A deep feeling undoubtedly pervades the whole Commonwealth, that this ancient and venerable University ought never to be permitted to become a mere sectarian Institution, and that no new door should be opened for giving undue preponderance to any special theological views. The undersigned sympathize sincerely and strongly with this feeling, and they would be among the last persons in the community to give their sanction to the contemplated Professorship, if it were intended to be employed in securing an additional predominance to any one religious denomination.

But there is, they believe, a feeling not less deep, nor less pervading, in Massachusetts, that a greater measure of religious influence than now exists, is essential to the welfare of our seminaries of learning, and of the University at Cambridge as one of them, and that some new measures may well be devised for this end. The Overseers themselves, through their Visiting Committee, have, at two successive annual meetings of the Board, given expression to their opinion upon this subject, and have commended it to the particular attention of the Corporation. On one occasion, this was done in the form of solemn Resolutions in the following words:

"Resolved, That there is need of more direct religious influence in the College.

"Resolved, That the Corporation be requested to take immediate measures to supply the same."

These Resolutions were the result of long and

careful deliberation by a sub-committee combining gentlemen of almost every variety of religious and political connection,—consisting of Hon. Edward Everett, Hon. George S. Boutwell, Rev. Dr. Gannett, Rev. R. A. Miller, and Rev. Dr. Sears,—and they were unanimously adopted by the Visiting Committee, and accepted by the Overseers at the January meeting of 1854.

The death of Miss Caroline Plummer, of Salem, on the 15th of May following, and the devotion of so considerable a sum to the purpose prescribed in her Will, at the very moment when the Corporation must have been at a loss how to proceed in complying with the recommendation of the Overseers for want of precisely such a foundation,—is, to say the least, a very striking coincidence. Our Puritan Fathers, by whom the College was founded, would have regarded it as something more than a fortunate accident, and would have given it a place in their catalogue of remarkable providences.

But it would certainly be a not less striking fact, if, under all these circumstances, the Overseers should now find cause for declining the bequest, rejecting the foundation, and receding from their own twice repeated recommendations.

In the opinion of the undersigned, the proposed foundation is one which meets those precise wants of the College which were aimed at by the Overseers in their resolutions of January, 1854, and which were again urged upon the attention of the Corporation, in the Annual Report of the Visiting Committee of the present year. Nothing can be plainer, than that the object of the Testatrix was to provide for "a more direct religious influence in the College," and to do this, not through the medium of recitations and lectures, by which the intellect only should be sharpened and disciplined for religious speculation and theological controversy,—but by such exercises and appeals as should reach the heart and the life, promoting generous affections, manly virtues and Christian conduct and character. Christianity, and not sectarianism; pure and undefiled religion, and not dogmatic theology; the faith of the gospel of Christ, and the virtues which are its legitimate fruits, and not scientific creeds or human ceremonials;—these were unmistakably in the contemplation of the excellent lady by whom this Professorship was provided for; and nothing other than these could have been in the minds of the Overseers, when they urged upon the Corporation the need of more direct religious influence in the College.

It is an interesting fact in this connection, and one which should not be lost to the history of the question, that the original idea, and the precise language of the foundation under consideration, were derived from a discourse delivered many years ago, before the Alumni of Harvard, by one of the most respected of their number, who was for a long time a member of this Board, and who still lives to witness the result of his timely suggestion.

In the address of the Hon. Daniel Appleton White, of Salem, delivered at the second celebration of the Association of the Alumni, on the 27th of August, 1844, will be found the following passages:

"We rejoice in every act which raises the dignity and extends the usefulness of our time-honored University. Her professional schools are public blessings. That of the Law, the most recently established, cannot fail to be instrumental in spreading through the country those sound and broad principles of jurisprudence, not unmingled with New England influence, which are the safeguard of the Constitution and the Federal Union. If need be, let a School of Philosophy be added, which may answer the wish, sometimes expressed, that every American College might be a sort of Lowell Institute to the region in which it is placed. But let our *Alma Mater* never forget her first love ; let nothing ever interfere with her original and main design, the education of youth, the training up of wise and good men and ripe scholars, to be guides of their countrymen and ornaments of mankind.

"'*Out of the heart are the issues of life.*' The wisest philosophers and teachers, of all ages and nations, Gentile, Jew and Christian, Plato and Plutarch, not less than Solomon and Paul, have attached the highest importance to moral culture, to the training of the young in the way in which they should go.

"Nor is this doctrine confined to professed teachers and philosophers. Profound and practical jurists, who, in the course of their studies and duties, take the keenest glances into human nature, still more emphatically proclaim it. 'Nothing,' says an eminent English justice, of the last century, 'is more pestilent than powers of intellect undisciplined by virtue.' A more eminent justice of the United States, *chief* justice really, if not *executively*, inculcating, in his address to a grand jury, the indispensable necessity of morals and intelligence to a republican people, declares, in a loftier tone and with characteristic energy, that intellect disunited from morals operates like a tornado, destroying every thing in its course, to accomplish its own selfish and wicked purposes.' " . . . . .

" Let the next foundation laid here in aid of education be, a *Professorship of the Philosophy of the Heart and the Moral Life.* Would not light emanate from such a source to guide in their duties all who are connected with the University—legislators, governors, teachers, students, Alumni? Might not a lofty and pervading spirit be diffused, uniting all more clearly, more earnestly, and more intelligently in their aims and efforts to educate the true man, as well as to produce the fine scholar?"

In little more than six months from the delivery of these sentiments, and while they were still fresh from the press, the original codicil containing the bequest under consideration was prepared and executed; and the merest comparison of dates and language would be abundantly sufficient, even were other testimony wanting, to establish the identity of views between the author of the Address and his estimable friend and neighbor by whom the Professorship was founded.

The undersigned need hardly add, after what has thus been said, that they see nothing of evil to be apprehended, but, on the contrary, every thing of good to be hoped, from the establishment of such a Professorship, and that they, therefore, cordially recommend to the Overseers a concurrence with the Corporation in the acceptance of the bequest, upon the terms and conditions, and to the trusts, purposes and intent, expressed in the codicil which has been heretofore recited.

II. The second question involved in the record of the Corporation which has been referred to your Committee, relates to the particular Rules and Statutes which are proposed for the Plummer Professorship.

These are few and simple, and seem to the undersigned to be every way adapted to fulfill the purposes of the founder, and to promote the welfare of the University.

The first and principal duty which they assign to the new Professor, is that of conducting the religious services of the University, including at once the daily devotional exercises of the chapel, and the public worship of the Sabbath. In this respect, as need only be suggested, the Statutes provide rather for a transfer of existing duties, than for the creation of any new ones. The daily prayers and weekly worship of the University are now mainly conducted by the Professors of the Cambridge Theological School, who are paid for these extra-official services out of the general College funds. It seems to be understood that this school will soon be entirely divorced from the University ; and, even should this long-desired event be still further delayed, it can hardly fail to be more satisfactory to the Overseers, and to the community, that the religious exercises of the College should be under the charge of a single Professor selected with special reference to this particular duty, rather than that they should be left to the joint or to the alternate care of several Professors, however able or faithful, who are connected with a sectarian Seminary, and whose particular province may be to give instruction in dogmatic Theology.

But apart from either of these views, it seems to the undersigned intrinsically fit and proper, that a Professor who is to have the peculiar care of the moral character and culture of the students, should be charged also with conducting the religious exercises of the University. In no other way could he hope to fulfill the purposes of his appointment so effectually. It is, moreover, a becoming and just recognition of the great truth, that there is no safe separation between morals and religion;—a truth which the Father of his Country thought it not inappropriate to commend so earnestly to attention in these memorable words of his Farewell Address:

"And let us with caution indulge the supposition, that morality can be maintained without religion. Whatever may be conceded to the influence of refined education on minds of peculiar structure, reason and experience both forbid us to expect that national morality can prevail in exclusion of religious principles."

The undersigned would have had little confidence in the success of the Plummer Foundation, and little disposition to vindicate it from the objections which have been arrayed against it, if the Statutes had not provided that the Professor should be privileged, and should be required, to avail himself of every appropriate opportunity for bringing the sanctions of religion, and the precepts of the Bible, in aid of any moral influences which he may attempt to exert, or of any moral instruction which he may be called on to impart.

Nor have they the slightest reason to doubt, that such an arrangement is entirely consistent with the intentions of the founder. Miss Caroline Plummer had plainly no idea of providing for the propagation of any mere philosophical morality. It was "Christian character," on the basis of "Christian faith and love," which she desired and directed her Professor to promote. And how are Christian faith and love to be promoted and inculcated, without the exercises of religion and the observance of the Sabbath?

The other duties which are assigned to this Professor by the Rules and Statutes under consideration are more general in their nature, and such only as are distinctly expressed, or substantially indicated in the Will of the founder. With regard to these, therefore, there can be no question, if the bequest is to be accepted.

The undersigned were disposed to doubt at first, whether the tenure of office prescribed in the Statutes was in exact accordance with the language of the Testatrix, which declares that the Professor "shall be elected by the President and Fellows, and approved by the Overseers of Harvard College *for such a term of years* as may, by them, be ordered." And there might still be room for a question whether these words do not require some limitation of the general tenure by which the Professors on other foundations hold their office. As this, however, is a matter of technical legal construction, which could not have been adopted by the Corporation without passing under the consideration of the highest judicial authority in the State, your Committee have not been disposed to raise an issue upon it,—more especially as they entirely concur in the expediency of the tenure prescribed by the Statutes.

Two questions have, however, been brought into discussion in the course of their deliberations, upon which they feel bound to say a few words before bringing their Report to a close.

It has been suggested, in the first place, that the establishment of this Professorship is an interference with the Hollis Professorship of Divinity, and that certainly there can be no occasion for a new foundation of this sort while that Professorship remains vacant.

The undersigned have no intention of entering at any length into the vexed subject of the Hollis Professorship. The responsibility of initiating all measures upon this and other Professorships rests exclusively upon the Corporation, and your Committee do not feel called upon to pronounce judgment upon the policy which the Corporation have thought fit to pursue, either in filling the Hollis Professorship heretofore, or in leaving it vacant now. But they cannot omit to say that, in their humble opinion, the two Professorships are entirely different and distinct in their nature and objects. The Hollis Professorship is emphatically a Theological Professorship, and the first and principal duty of the Professor is "to instruct the students in the several parts of Theology by reading a system of positive, and a course of controversial Divinity." It can hardly be denied, too, that the Hollis Professorship is, in some sense and to some extent, a sectarian Professorship,—notwithstanding the liberal and catholic views of its benevolent and excellent founder, for the period in which he lived. His own statutes provide that no one can be appointed to the Professorship who is not "in communion with some Christian Church of one of the three denominations, Congregational, Presbyterian, or Baptist." Now it might be difficult to say how many of the existing religious denominations of the world are included by such a definition, but it is obvious to everybody that more than one of them would be *excluded*.

It is true, that by a vote passed by the Corporation and Overseers in 1804, it was made "the duty of the Hollis Professor of Divinity to preach, and to perform other divine services in the chapel, before the officers, graduates and undergraduates, on the Lord's Day, forenoon and afternoon, whenever the same shall be hereafter required by the Corporation and Overseers." But this duty was expressly dependent upon the pleasure of the two bodies which passed it. It was no part of the duties prescribed by Hollis in his own statutes. On the contrary, it may well be doubted whether it was not in direct contravention of those statutes, which, after providing for lectures on "positive, controversial and casuistical Divinity," and for answering the questions of the students "on cases of conscience or controversies of religion," go on expressly to declare that "the Professor of Divinity, while in office, shall not be a tutor in any other science, or *obliged to any other attendance in the College than the above-mentioned Public and Private Lectures.*"

The undersigned can perceive no conflict or interference whatever between the legitimate duties of the Hollis Professorship, whenever it shall again be filled, or of any other existing Professorship, and those of the new Professor on the Plummer Foundation.

It has been suggested, in the second place, that the bequest of Miss Plummer is insufficient for the support of her Professorship, and that the duties assigned to it cannot be rightfully paid for, in whole or in part, out of the Academic Funds.

Now no question about salary has been submitted to the action of the Overseers. But it is quite too plain to be denied or overlooked, that neither *five* per cent., nor *six* per cent., upon Fifteen Thousand Dollars, would be an adequate salary for the Professorship now in contemplation. It cannot be doubted, therefore, that some portion of that salary is to be paid out of the general funds of the College, and the Overseers are not at liberty to close their eyes to this fact in giving their assent to the establishment of the Professorship. But the undersigned can find no ground of objection to the measure on this account. The religious exercises of the College have always been a charge upon the Academic funds, to a greater or less extent, and they always ought to be, until some other and sufficient funds are provided for the purpose. At the present moment, as has already been stated, the Professors of the Theological School are paid from the common treasury of the University for conducting the very services which are now to be transferred to the Plummer Professor, and a considerable sum is also paid from the same source for providing accommodations in other churches in Cambridge for those students whose parents or guardians do not wish them to attend Sunday worship in the College chapel.

It would certainly be desirable that the general funds of the College should be relieved from these charges, if separate and adequate foundations existed, or could be supplied, for the purpose. But it will hardly be contended on any side, that the daily or the weekly worship of God should be altogether abandoned, and all religious exercises discontinued, until special endowments for this exclusive object shall have been obtained. This would be to reverse the whole usage of the University during two centuries and a quarter of honored and prosperous existence. It would be to reverse the whole propriety and fitness of things in such an Institution. In the opinion of the undersigned, the worship of God is the first thing, and not the last thing, to be provided for, in a great seminary of learning ; and the religious instructions of the Sabbath are as much a part of any true system of education as the recitations and lectures of the week-day.

The particular management of the funds of the College, and the whole appropriation of salaries, have for a long course of years been left exclusively to the Corporation. How far it might be in the power of the Overseers to control them in this matter, is a question which it is not necessary to consider on this occasion. But if there be any thing which, in the opinion of the undersigned, would demand the interposition of this Board to the full extent of its powers, it would be the failure of the Corporation to make adequate provision, out of the general funds of the College, for supplying any deficiency which may exist in the means which may have been specially appropriated to maintaining the stated devotional exercises of the chapel. Harvard College would hardly know itself,—its founders, were they still in the flesh, would disown it,—good men everywhere would renounce all respect for it and all relations with it, if no voice of morning or evening prayer or praise were to be heard within its halls, and no guidance and guardianship of Wisdom from above were to be daily or nightly implored, for those who, at so critical a period of their lives, are withdrawn from the parental roof, and gathered within its gates.

The undersigned esteem it a subject for special congratulation, that a foundation has at length been laid, which will render these services perpetual. It has come with peculiar grace and beauty, as the pious tribute of a true-hearted sister to the memory of a beloved brother. That such a bequest should be rejected, or that it should be received with anything but cordial gratitude, by either branch of the College government, is hardly to be credited. It is easy, indeed, to speculate upon the injurious influences which might result from the perversion of such a foundation, and to conjure up forms of evil or of wrong which might be produced by its intentional abuse. It must be acknowledged, too, that the measure is to a certain degree experimental in some of its features, and that its ultimate results must depend on the discretion, devotion, and fidelity with which it shall be carried out. But no one will deny that it is an experiment in the right direction,—that it is eminently worthy of being tried, and that the blessing of Heaven may be confidently invoked for its success.

The undersigned, for themselves, have no hesitation in welcoming the Plummer Foundation, as now proposed to be established, and in connection with the erection of the new Chapel, for which means have been recently provided by the munificence of a late esteemed and respected Boston merchant, as affording a promise and an assurance of improvements in the condition of the University, which should be hailed with the highest satisfaction by all who are interested in its best welfare.

With these views they conclude by offering the following resolutions to the consideration of the Board:

Resolved, That the Overseers do cordially and gratefully concur with the Corporation in the acceptance of the bequest of the late Miss Caroline Plummer, and in the establishment of a new Professorship agreeably to the terms of that bequest.

Resolved, That the Overseers do assent to "the Rules and Statutes of the office of Preacher to the

University and Plummer Professor of Christian Morals," which have been submitted to them by the Corporation.

All which is respectfully submitted by

ROBERT C. WINTHROP,
SIMON BROWN,
ABBOTT LAWRENCE,
THOMAS RUSSELL.

Boston, April 11, 1855.

The foregoing Report having been read and debated at length, the question on the two Resolutions was taken separately and by Yeas and Nays, as follows:

On the first Resolution,

YEAS,—His Honor the Lieut. Governor, the President of the University, the Treasurer of the University, Hon. Daniel W. Alvord, Hon. Robert C. Winthrop, Rev. Dr. Gannett, Hon. Samuel Hoar, Hon. David Sears, Hon. Abbott Lawrence, Rev. Thomas Worcester, Hon. Francis Bassett, Hon. George S. Boutwell, Hon. Samuel D. Bradford, Rev. S. M. Worcester, D. D., Rev. Dr. Blagden, Rev. Nathaniel Cogswell, Hon. George Morey, Hon. Thomas Russell, Hon. Emory Washburn, Hon. Henry B. Wheelwright, Hon. N. B. Shurtleff,—21.

NAYS, The President of the Senate, Rev. Rodney A. Miller,—2.

On the second Resolution,

YEAS,—His Honor the Lieut. Governor, the President of

the University, the Treasurer of the University, Hon. Robert C. Winthrop, Rev. Dr. Gannett, Hon. Samuel Hoar, Hon. David Sears, Hon. Abbott Lawrence, Rev. Thomas Worcester, Hon. Francis Bassett, Hon. George S. Boutwell, Rev. Samuel M. Worcester, D. D., Rev. Dr. Blagden, Rev. Nathaniel Cogswell, Hon. George Morey, Hon. Thomas Russell, Hon. Emory Washburn, Hon. Henry B. Wheelwright, Hon. N. B. Shurtleff,—19.

Nays,—The President of the Senate, Hon. Daniel W. Alvord, Rev. Rodney A. Miller, Hon. Samuel D. Bradford,—4.

The Resolutions reported by the Committee having thus been adopted, the following additional Resolution was then moved by the Rev. Dr. Blagden:

Resolved, That, provided the necessary funds be offered, the Hollis Professorship, in the opinion of the Board, ought to be filled in accordance with the intention of the founder.

The Yeas and Nays having been ordered, the Resolution was adopted, as follows:

Yeas,—His Honor the Lieut. Governor, the President of the Senate, the Treasurer of the University, Hon. Daniel W. Alvord, Rev. Rodney A. Miller, Hon. Robert C. Winthrop, Hon. Samuel Hoar, Hon. David Sears, Hon. Abbott Lawrence, Rev. Thomas Worcester, Hon. Francis Bassett, Hon. George S. Boutwell, Hon. Samuel D. Bradford, Rev. Samuel M. Worcester, D. D., Rev. Dr. Blagden, Rev. Nathaniel Cogswell, Hon. George Morey, Hon. Thomas Russell, Hon. Emory Washburn, Hon. Henry B. Wheelwright, Hon. N. B. Shurtleff,—20.

Nays,—0.

The President of the University, Rev. Dr. Gannett, and Rev. Dr. Ballou were excused from voting for reasons given.

The question was then taken on concurring with the Corporation, in the appointment of the Rev. Frederick D. Huntington as Preacher to the University and Plummer Professor of Christian Morals, when it appeared that the whole number of ballots was 24, of which 22 were in the affirmative, and 2 in the negative, and there was one blank. The nomination of the Rev. Frederick D. Huntington was accordingly declared to be confirmed.

www.ingramcontent.com/pod-product-compliance
Lightning Source LLC
LaVergne TN
LVHW011141110826
845150LV00008B/2456

* 9 7 8 1 4 1 8 1 9 2 7 6 1 *